Practical Toilet Training: Successful Strategies for Children on the Spectrum

Written by Sabrina Verost, M.A. Ed and Edited by Monife G. Stout, M.A.

Published by Sabrina Verost, M.S. Ed, 2024.

Table of Contents

This publication is designed to provide accurate and authoritative information in regard to the subject matter covered. It is sold with the understanding that the author is not engaged in rendering legal, investment, accounting or other professional services. While the author has used their best efforts in preparing this book, they make no representations or warranties with respect to the accuracy or completeness of the contents of this book and specifically disclaim any implied warranties of merchantability or fitness for a particular purpose. No warranty may be created or extended by sales representatives or written sales materials. The advice and strategies contained herein may not be suitable for your situation. You should consult with a professional when appropriate. Neither the publisher nor the author shall be liable for any loss of profit or any other commercial damages, including but not limited to special, incidental, consequential, personal, or other damages.

DISCLAIMER: The views expressed in the book do not necessarily represent the views of the Department of Education or the City of New York.

Cover Design: Sabrina Verost, M.S. Ed

Editor: Monife G. Stout, M.A.: monife.stout@gmail.com

Special Thanks:

First, I must thank God,

who in His amazing ability to use our talents to benefit others, has given me discretion in the area of toilet training.

I'd like to thank all the educators, therapists and paraprofessionals that have worked with me for over 15 years. They have supported my vision to toilet train children on the Spectrum and encouraged me to never give up. Thank you to Yaccovia Davis,

the young woman of faith and vision who encouraged me to take this skill to another level and share it with the world.

I'd like to thank Jori O'Neale for starting my writing momentum. Thank you as well to Monife Stout for organizing my thoughts.

A special thanks to Robin Edwards and her husband for mentoring me over the years as I worked providing services to their daughter, Thailyn.

This book is dedicated to my 3 heartbeats,

Maya, Dante and Jaiden.

My hope is that generations read this book and successfully toilet train their children in my memory.

Finally,

I must thank the man that has kept his promise to make every day of my life with him an adventure,

my husband and best friend,

Ryan Verost.

Introduction: Why toilet training?

THE GOAL OF THIS BOOK is to help members of the autism community (educators, parents, guardians, and loved ones) to successfully toilet train a child who has been diagnosed with **autism spectrum disorder (ASD)**. It is my hope that this book will equip you with the tools, strategies and encouragement to persevere through this process.

Describing this process as "toilet training" as opposed to "potty training" is deliberate to help you transition your language to match the child's age. Using age-appropriate words with children on the Spectrum is crucial to their development as they approach pre-teen age and adolescence.

As a special education instructor, my daily routine is to individualize the curriculum for each of my students. My tasks include, but are not limited to, implementing their **Individualized Educational Program (IEP)**, creating visual schedules to help the children navigate their day, and using educational materials to help them achieve their individual instructional goals. I also create learning centers, provide behavior management (to help regulate behavioral needs) and delegate responsibilities for the paraprofessionals who support my vision for the class.

I have over 20 years of experience working with children with ASD; and I have learned that children have universal behaviors, although no two children are exactly alike. The **Applied Behavior**

Analysis (ABA) based techniques explained in this book will work for most elementary-age children, if the person conducting the toilet training is consistent and deliberate.

As you begin, or revisit, the toilet training process, it is important to know that you are not alone. Every school year I have helped a child with autism and their family navigate the challenges of toilet training and experience success. Yes, there is help for you and if you have the tiniest seed of faith, you can witness a miracle. As my team and I have watched the effectiveness of toilet training strategies and techniques unfold, we can proclaim... "It is a modern-day miracle!"

Use the reflective aspects located at the end of each chapter to keep track of your thoughts as you go through this journey with the child you are training. A sample data sheet and a generic toileting **social story** for your personalization are included through my Teachers Pay Teachers (TPT) account using the provided QR code in Chapter 11. Be vulnerable with your thoughts and maintain a positive mindset.

Chapter 1: Where are you on your toilet training journey?

INITIAL STEPS IN ACHIEVING success in toilet training children who have been diagnosed with ASD is acknowledging the pain associated with the diagnosis and moving forward by embracing all the beautiful attributes of your child. This unique experience you will have with them requires that you understand the child you are training. Your care for your child will motivate you to endure the challenges as you help them learn to communicate, be independent, and have a thriving, meaningful life full of happiness and love.

The child you are training needs you to have new hopes and dreams for them. They need you to create and organize goals that will help them develop life skills. Using set goals will guide you through the daily, weekly, and monthly process as the child develops.

Having support is crucial to your success in training a child on the Spectrum, so I urge you to connect with families who are in similar situations through the child's school and agencies in your community that may be resourceful. Early intervention is key on the toilet training journey, so being part of a community will help you to positively impact a child's life and take advantage of the opportunity to successfully toilet train your child.

Chapter 1 Reflection Questions:

WHO CAN YOU PARTNER with to help you reach your toilet training goal (ex: teachers, pediatricians, etc.)?

WITH WHOM CAN YOU SHARE your toilet training dilemma?

Chapter 2: Let's toilet train!

Wait...what? The child is not ready!

UNDERSTANDING THE SIGNS of readiness to begin toilet training a child is crucial to ensuring the child maintains a positive attitude toward the process. Instituting toilet training for a child on the Spectrum when they are experiencing emotional challenges or are physically incapable, will associate toilet training with something adverse or negative.

What are the physical readiness signs for toilet training?
Physical signs of toilet training readiness include:

- staying dry for a period of time
- sticking to a regular pattern of bowel movements
- having the ability to get to the toilet
- being able to pull pants on and off with and without assistance
- sitting down on the toilet with and without assistance.

Below are some excerpts from the article titled "Signs of Toilet Training Readiness: When to start, and when to wait," Gwen Dewar (2021) from *Parenting Science*.

Back in 1999, Dr. Peter Gorski presented a set of signs which are still embraced by the American Academy of Pediatrics today. He advised that kids should be capable of:

- *imitating your actions*

- *putting some objects 'where they belong'*

- *showing independence by saying 'no'*

- *expressing an interest in toilet training (by, for instance, following you into the bathroom)*

- *walking and sitting down*

- *communicating when they are urinating or defecating, and when they need to do these things*

- *removing and replacing their clothes (i.e., pulling their pants up and down).*

In addition, physician Drew Baird and colleagues (2019) suggest that parents look for signs that children are:

- *demonstrating 'dissatisfaction' with a dirty diaper (i.e., they want to stay clean, and feel distressed by soiled or wet diapers)*

- *using 'expressive' language*

- *showing 'bladder or bowel control' (e.g., staying dry for two hours at a time, or during a nap).*

And other experts have proposed more signs of toilet training readiness, including:

PRACTICAL TOILET TRAINING: SUCCESSFUL STRATEGIES FOR CHILDREN ON THE SPECTRUM

- *asking to use a potty chair, or to wear 'big kid' underwear; (American Academy of Family Physicians, 2019)*

- *responding to directions, questions or explanations (Wyndaele, et al., 2020)*

- *wanting to perform tasks independently, and showing pride in such achievements (O'Connell, 2000; Schum, et al., 2002)*

- *displaying a desire to control elimination, and actively participate in toilet training (Canadian Pediatric Society, 2000; Schum, et al., 2002).*

Limitations in toilet training:
In general, you shouldn't try to begin toilet training unless the child is:

- *healthy (no diarrhea or constipation, for example)*
- *relaxed (not stressed by new life changes, for instance, a move)*
- *cooperative (not going through a rebellious phase).*

Let's remember that children on the Spectrum learn differently from other children. If you want to introduce the concept of toilet training, you can start with:

- Reading books about toilet training a child on the Spectrum and using social stories as referenced in Chapter 11 will be helpful. Social stories offer verbal and visual explanations of difficult situations about toilet training and provide a resolution at the end of each story.

- Introduce underwear or have the underwear over the pull-up.

- Allow them to see siblings that are successfully using the toilet.

Chapter 2 Reflection Questions:

IF THE CHILD IS SHOWING some signs of readiness, then make a determination to start toilet training.

WHAT ARE THE PROS AND cons of starting the toilet training process?

Chapter 3: First, observe and gather data.

OBSERVING, DOCUMENTING, and/or dating the following behaviors are the first steps to toilet training after the child exhibits some signs of readiness:

- What **reinforcements** does the child prefer?

- Where (what part of the house) does the child prefer to urinate or defecate in their diaper?

- Is he or she asking for diapers or managing the diapers themselves?

- If you take off their diaper, how do they respond to wetting themselves?

- At what time of day do they have soiled diapers?

- Do they enjoy certain drinks?

- Do they show signs of needing to urinate or defecate while in their diaper?

- When eliminating in their diaper, do they stay quiet, pause, or hide?

- Do they cross their legs, touch their crotch or have a certain facial expression when they are about to soil their diaper?

- Does your child wake up dry or saturated in the morning?

Noticing patterns in your observations will be helpful in the next step of the toilet training process.

Chapter 3 Reflection Questions:

WHAT HAVE YOU OBSERVED based on the questions in this chapter?

WHAT ARE THE NOTABLE patterns?

Chapter 4: Setting the scene!

WHETHER YOU ARE IN the home or in the classroom, you have to set up your space for the inevitable... toilet training accidents. Start by:

- Familiarize the child with wearing underwear.

- Have the child wear underwear over their pull-ups or diapers even if it's for half of the day.

- Drinks must be administered with

the understanding that one of two things will happen within the following hour: either you will observe the child urinating in the toilet or on themselves. Either way, it's a win!

- Reinforce them and start the process of associating urinating in the toilet with something good, if they urinate in the toilet. Observe how they react to the feeling of being wet. Are they uncomfortable or disgusted? Do they look at you in shock? Is there no reaction?

This is also the time to:

- Roll up your area rugs.

- Cover your couch with plastic.
- Gather paper towels, gloves, disinfectant wipes and a cleaning spray.
- Have extra underwear, pants, socks and a shirt ready.

The first couple of days may be a bit messy. In between accidents, they will sit on the toilet fairly frequently based on the **intervals** you have selected. It might sound extreme, but I suggest toilet training every 5-10 minutes for the first few days until the child understands what is expected.

The child should start to eventually hold their urine because they dislike the feeling of being wet. Now your job is to observe them urinating in the toilet and give them positive reinforcement every time. This will build the mental connection of using the toilet with reinforcement. Remember to have them continually sipping their liquid of choice! If they don't drink, they will not have the urge to urinate.

Chapter 4 Reflection Questions:

HOW DOES YOUR CHILD behave when not wearing a diaper?

HOW DOES THE CHILD react when he/she has a toileting accident?

WHAT ARE YOUR OBSERVATIONS?

ARE THERE ANY PATTERNS? Explain.

Chapter 5: What would you like to drink?

THERE WAS A TIME DURING my journey of toilet training my students when I noticed they were not urinating. Feeling stuck, I asked a colleague who reminded me that the amount of liquid a child drinks will affect whether or not they urinate. Empty bladder means an empty toilet. I then asked parents to bring their child's favorite drink with them to class, ensured the children got their fill, set the timer and waited.

Low sugar drinks are always a good option, and if your child loves water, equip them with an ample supply. Have them sip on fluids and put them on the toilet every five to ten minutes from 9AM to 12PM (half the day). Give yourself permission to start slowly and increase the intervals as needed. Please be mindful not to over hydrate the child you are toilet training.

To begin, use a timer and seat the child on the toilet for five minutes then have them return to their activities. Keep all activities close to the toilet during this training period. A timer is crucial to the consistency of toilet training.

The goal is for the child to drink fluids while not wearing a diaper then sit on the toilet after the timer goes off. This can be a repetitive process before the child actually urinates in the toilet. Keep in mind your child will have accidents, and your reaction to those accidents matters most. Being neutral and not reacting in frustration or in anger is crucial to the child having a pleasant toileting experience. Use subtle positive reinforcement to help the child associate toileting with a desirable behavior.

You must also be positive and believe they will urinate. It may seem impossible at the time, but if you are negative and believe "this will never happen," then it won't. Your attitude, whether positive or negative, will be reflected in your actions, and you may not even notice it.

The next chapter will further explain the benefit of having positive reactions during toilet training.

Chapter 5 Reflection Questions:

HOW IS THE CHILD TOLERATING sipping drinks?

WHAT ARE THE POSITIVE/negative attitudes you are having towards toileting accidents?

IN THE EVENT THAT YOUR attitude/tone or actions are negative, what can you do to train yourself to react neutrally?

Chapter 6: Why would a child want to use the bathroom?

FOR **reinforcers**!

Once your child urinates in the toilet, even accidentally, using this opportunity to reinforce their action with a small reward including praise or a small tangible item they favor is essential to success in training. Whether allowing them to watch a few minutes of their favorite TV show, or giving them a small snack or lick of a lollipop, a small reward is optimal to avoid losing the opportunity for them to associate voiding in the toilet as good. If the reward is too grand in any way (an entire bag of chips or lollipop), they may become **satiated**, scared, or startled and not repeat the action of using the toilet. The methods you use, as well as how you use them, will determine whether the behaviors are repeated. Perception is key to determining the right reinforcement for the child you are training.

What if my child does not want to go to the bathroom or sit on the toilet?

This is the time to use toys and lollipops and ration access to these items to control the training. Offering one lick of a lollipop as the child enters the bathroom, then another lick as they sit on the toilet, and a few licks if they sit on the toilet for five minutes or the length of the timer is key to success. Other ideas involve allowing your child to play with a toy while sitting on the toilet for the duration of the timer, or singing songs, counting, reading a book to distract the child, making the process safe and fun until they 'accidentally' urinate. The reward may now be numerous licks of a lollipop (not consuming the whole candy) and affirmative words followed by sending a farewell to the urine after flushing. This whole process can take days or weeks, so don't lose hope!

Social or verbal reinforcers, such as "good job," may suffice altogether or even as you fade out the tangibles. Eliminating in the toilet will ideally and eventually replace the **tangible reinforcers** because it's cleaner, and it feels good to have an empty bladder and bowel.

The reinforcer you choose must be highly desirable *and used only for toilet training*. If you use what they really like for other things, it will no longer motivate them to use the toilet. Children are very intelligent; they will not be motivated if they know they can get their reward later or from another person. I've used a variety of treats, and sometimes even offered the lick of a lollipop. You may think that it's too small, but in order for the child to want to get more they have to have a reason to go back and do it again, right? If not, as I mentioned before, satiation will occur too quickly. That means that you gave them so much of the thing that they like, that they are not motivated to work for it again. Essentially, they get content with what you gave them. You don't want that. You want the child to desire that wonderful piece of candy or treat again, so you give them small amounts every time they urinate.

Chapter 6 Reflection Questions:

WHAT SMALL REWARD CAN you give the child you are toilet training that will motivate them to urinate again in the toilet?

LIST SOME REINFORCERS you can use.

WHAT ARE YOUR THOUGHTS at this stage of the process?

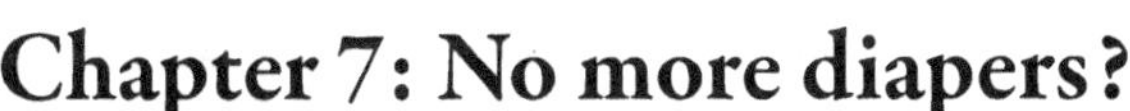

Chapter 7: No more diapers?

AT THIS POINT IN TOILET training, your focus should be developing consistency and routine as soon as the diaper on your child is removed. Establish intervals between the number of times you will take your child to the bathroom starting with shorter intervals. If you are ready to train then you can begin toileting every five minutes for half of the day.

The best thing you can do is start with shorter intervals and then work your way up to longer ones. I suggest five-minute intervals in the classroom or home from 8AM to 12PM. It seems painstaking, but it's usually a short window of time before the child realizes your goal.

If you do this five-minute interval, make sure to have the following in place:

- **Liquid of choice** for the child to sip on constantly – a must!

- A bag of treats (or a reinforcer of your choice – it should be something quick and small), just in case they urinate in the toilet and you need to reinforce it. (I have used a fanny pack to stash my reinforcers.) This is ESSENTIAL! You must reinforce the desired behavior, which is urinating in the toilet, right away so that the child will desire to do it again. Eventually, they *will* understand that *if* I urinate, *then* I get a treat – and it feels good to stay dry!

• Rolled up carpets/area rugs, covered couches, gloves and cleaning products for anticipated messes.

• A timer - another essential. Without the timer five minutes will pass by and the child will most likely have an accident. I've tried not using a timer many times, only to be frustrated with myself when the child has an accident. I missed my opportunity to catch them urinating in the toilet and to reinforce them.

• You can also use the timer to measure how long they sit on the toilet. Use your judgment, but always supervise them to ensure they don't stay on the toilet for more than approximately 7 minutes waiting for them to urinate.

• Finally, employ a mindset, attitude and behavior that reflects endurance. Patience is the cherry on top.

Do not scold or punish the child if they haven't yet made the connection between the urge to urinate or have a bowel movement and toileting. If you become frustrated, put the child in a diaper and reinforce them with a snack for trying. Do not use the specific treats or reinforcer you chose for a successful void. Seek out support, and try again another day.

Chapter 7 Reflection Questions:

BASED ON WHAT YOU'VE learned, what will be your toileting plan?

WITH WHAT TIME INTERVAL will you start toileting? (ex: Every 5 min, 10 min, 15 min, etc.) Remember, use a timer!

Chapter 8: Home stretch!

ONCE THE CHILD HAS been successfully dry for five to ten minutes, is able to void in the toilet, and you are reinforcing every success for a couple of days, you can increase the interval from 10 to 15 minutes. If the child is successful with that interval for a few days, then increase to 20 minutes. Follow the same trend (increasing five to ten minutes each time) until the child is able to hold their urine for a half hour and then eventually an hour.

Your child may have some accidents which are not failures but learning experiences. The child will not like to feel wet, so avoid changing the child right away and explain to them what happened *without scolding them*. Have the child sit on the toilet after the accident to allow them to empty their bladder. If they urinate after an accident, reinforce them as you regularly would. The act of allowing them to sit on the toilet and empty their bowels will show them some grace during the toileting accident. Most children on the Spectrum have communication delays, so the grace we grant them in teaching these new concepts will motivate them to do better through the toileting process. Sometimes, it may be helpful to backtrack and have them toilet at shorter intervals to help them avoid having an accident (every half hour or every 45 minutes if they are not ready for an hour).

WRITTEN BY SABRINA VEROST, M.A. ED AND EDITED BY MONIFE G. STOUT, M.A.

At this point, your child will have some understanding of what you're trying to achieve as independence is being established, which is freedom from wearing diapers. The finish line is in sight!

Chapter 8 Reflection Questions:

HOW CAN YOU DESCRIBE the child's growth regarding toilet training up to this point?

ARE ALL PARTIES BETWEEN home and school on the same page regarding toilet training?

IF NOT, WHAT STEPS can be taken to bridge that gap?

Chapter 9: Where do we go from here?

AS YOUR CHILD DEVELOPS the habit of relieving themselves on the toilet, the action will become a natural reinforcement ending the use of tangible mechanisms to encourage toileting.

<u>Things to consider:</u>

- As the child becomes comfortable holding their urine for a period of time and voiding in the toilet, pairing the toileting process with the phrase 'bathroom please!' and using a visual of a toilet to start the communicative process can begin.

- It is equally as important to implement modeling and teaching good hygiene, so they can learn to flush, and wash their hands after voiding as part of the entire toileting process.

At this point, you should have the child on some type of schedule. Have reinforcers readily available to link the action (urinating and/or even defecating in the toilet) with a desired consequence (a treat or toy and relief from holding their bowels). If the child voids in the toilet and you do not have a tangible reinforcer, that's fine! This is when you start giving them verbal praise and positive gestures.

For example:

- "Great job peeing/pooping in the toilet!"

- "Mom and/or dad are so proud of you for keeping your underwear clean and dry!"

- High fives

- Hugs

- Kisses

With time, the entire process will become part of the child's routine, even when you are not present.

Chapter 9 Reflection Questions:

LOOKING BACK ON THE past 9 chapters, how successful have you been in implementing all the strategies?

WHICH ONE DID YOU (or do you) find most difficult and why? See frequently asked questions in Chapter 10.

Chapter 10: Frequently asked questions (FAQ)

1. CAN I MAKE TOILET training an IEP goal for my child in school?

Absolutely! The following are a few ideas of IEP goals for a male and female child (please be mindful that the IEP format may be different for your particular school):

Long-Term Goal (1 year):

Given faded **prompts**, (student) will void in the toilet every hour, 4 out of 5 times, with 80% accuracy over the course of 2 weeks. Progress will be measured monthly by the special education teacher.

Short-Term Goals:
First Quarter:

Given visuals and faded physical prompts, (student) will void in the toilet within a 10-to-15-minute interval, 4 out of 5 times, with 80% accuracy over the course of 2 weeks. Progress will be monitored monthly by the special education teacher.

Second Quarter:

Given visuals and faded physical prompts, <u>(student)</u> will void in the toilet within a 15-to-30-minute interval, 4 out of 5 times, with 80% accuracy over the course of 2 weeks. Progress will be monitored monthly by the special education teacher.

Third Quarter:

Given visuals and faded physical prompts, <u>(student)</u> will void in the toilet within a 30-to-45-minute interval, 4 out 5 times, with 80% accuracy over the course of 2 weeks. Progress will be monitored monthly by the special education teacher.

What about a goal for a male that needs to learn to stand at the urinal?

The following is a sample of an IEP for a male learning how to stand at an urinal (assuming that he has learned to toilet train while seated and voids successfully every hour):

Long-Term Goal (1 Year):

Given faded prompts, <u>(student)</u> will void in the urinal with faded prompts by pulling down pants and aiming in the urinal every period, 4 out of 5 times, with 80% accuracy over the course of two weeks. Progress will be measured monthly by the special education teacher.

PRACTICAL TOILET TRAINING: SUCCESSFUL STRATEGIES FOR CHILDREN ON THE SPECTRUM

Short-Term Goals:

First Quarter:

Given visuals and faded physical prompts, <u>(student)</u> will void by standing at the urinal with *faded full assistance* by pulling down pants and aiming in the urinal, 4 out of 5 times, with 80% accuracy over the course of two weeks. Progress will be monitored monthly by the special education teacher.

Second Quarter:

Given visuals and faded physical prompts, <u>(student)</u> will void by standing at the urinal with *faded partial prompts* by pulling down pants and aiming in the urinal, 4 out of 5 times, with 80% accuracy over the course of two weeks. Progress will be monitored monthly by the special education teacher.

Third Quarter:

Given visuals and faded physical prompts, <u>(student)</u> will void by standing at the urinal with *faded gestures* by pulling down pants and aiming in the urinal, 4 out of 5 times, with 80% accuracy over the course of two weeks. Progress will be monitored monthly by the special education teacher.

2. What supplies are needed at school when my child is in the toilet training process?

Teachers will need five underwear and five pairs of pants

(at least) along with baby wipes and an extra pair of shoes. Teachers will also need juices along with water (as preferred by the parent). Fluids that the child enjoys will stimulate the need to urinate. I often suggest low-sugar juices.

3. How can you tell if the child is holding their urine?

You can tell a child is about to urinate simply by looking at their body language. Children who cross their legs, walk in an awkward way, or touch their genital area should be taken to the bathroom regardless of their toileting interval or the setting on their timer.

Once you observe them and reinforce them, you've won a battle, and you are helping them to make connections!

4. What do I do if the child is waiting to put on the diaper to urinate?

If he or she is waiting for the diaper, then you *know* they are aware of when they need to void. Have them drink ample amounts of fluids and start the interval timer. Once the timer goes off, take them to the bathroom and make it a fun and pleasant experience. You may run water in the sink, read their favorite book, give them access to sensory toys (playdoh, putty, fidgets), make them laugh, and be sure to have those reinforcers handy. A child that is fully aware of the toilet and its usage should have their social story read with them consistently. If this is successful, you will observe them urinating. It's important that when it happens, you keep praise at a low tone, as if it's not a huge deal (even though it is in your head). If your reaction is too big, you may distract them and they may stop urinating mid-stream or not completely empty their bladder. Quietly let them finish and then give them a reinforcer. It's nice to end a successful toileting moment by saying "Bye-bye pee!" and then flushing the toilet.

5. What if the child doesn't want to sit?

This is common, so find ways to reinforce the child when they do sit on the toilet. I have used lollipops and/or sensory toys for these situations. Have them sit on the toilet for a minute with a timer and when the timer goes off let them get a lick of the lollipop and say, "Great sitting!" Sometimes distractions, like a book or tablet, help as well. I know that may seem unsanitary, but it's a sacrifice that will pay off later. Using sanitizers and wipes to clean off surfaces will suffice. Sitting with them on a low stool or listening to music can also be reassuring.

These strategies will build up their tolerance for sitting. Over time, they will no longer see it as a scary place. Exercising perseverance is key as you grow through this process.

6. Can a child stay in a diaper in school and/or at home if toilet training?

Every child is different. You must learn the child with whom you are working. My motto is "the longer the child keeps the diaper on, the more normal urinating in a diaper will be for them."

When dealing with children on the Spectrum, routine and consistency are keys for learning – whether it be behaviors you want them to learn or those you want them to change. Most neurotypical children are toilet trained by the age of four. If you have a child on the Spectrum in a diaper, as they grow and develop past the age of five, they will be familiar with this "routine" and keep the habit because they have not learned otherwise.

In most cases, it is best to keep the child out of the diaper while at school.

Yes, there may be accidents.

Yes, the child will feel uncomfortable (which is good – another sign they are ready to train).

Yes, it's inconvenient.

Yes, you must always be ready with a change of clothes.

Yes, you must look for signs they need to use the toilet.

Yes, you may have to clean puddles.

Yes! All are sacrifices that are well worth it!

The inconveniences will be minimal if training is consistent with use of a routine, reinforcers, intervals, fluids, and reading bathroom ready stories. If your child is sick with loose bowels or your own stress levels are interfering with the toilet training process, then use of a diaper on the child is acceptable. At that time, you need to recharge and reach out to your support group (e.g., other parents, the special education team at your school, parent training, parent coordinators at your school, etc.).

7. What if my child or student resists the toilet training process?

Lean into your support groups and work with your child's teacher, family members, the babysitter etc. and read your child's social story on toileting daily. Make sure it is personalized with his or her name and picture. The social story provided through the QR code in Chapter 11 provides a page where you can add the child's picture and name. Again, sometimes this process needs to connect mentally before it develops physically. In addition to exposing your child to social stories about toilet training, be sure you are implementing the suggested strategies (see question 5) to make the process less intimidating for them.

8. Should a child toilet train in school if they are not toilet training at home or vice versa?

Yes! I have had children toilet train in school without the parents' support, and they are still able to **generalize** the skill at their home. Wherever you start the routine, that child will generalize it once given the opportunity.

Making this a success is all about starting the process.

One parent I worked with who had a child that was toilet trained at school put a diaper on the child while they went to the mall. She did not trust that her child could hold his urine outside of the home. To her surprise, he kept the diaper dry for two hours and urinated when he got home. The bottom line is that if you are consistent in any setting your toilet training efforts will not be in vain.

9. Can medication affect the toilet training process?

Possibly. Medication affects each child differently. A child in my classroom began using medication, and experienced severe constipation and frequent urination as side effects. The child soiled her pants a few times despite having been successfully toilet trained. However, there are other students whose use of medication never interfered with toilet training. The best thing to do is monitor your child for side effects, and stay in contact with your child's pediatrician.

10. What defines "success" in the toileting process?

Success can be as small as a squirt or dribble of urine in the toilet. Remember to give wait time for them to empty their bladder. The more comfortable they become with the process, the more urine they will void over time. Toileting should be viewed as a space for children to acquire positive reinforcement for any success.

Toilet training is complete when the child can consistently communicate their need to use the bathroom (using their preferred mode of communication), hold their urine until they reach a toilet, and urinate and/or empty their bowels successfully in a toilet. The use of symbols, communication devices, sign language, or any form of communication should always be encouraged and available for the child to use. It should be modeled throughout the process until the child is able to communicate in their own way.

11. My child or student doesn't drink juice or eat sweets. Can I still toilet train them successfully?

Yes, as long as they are drinking a consistent amount of water throughout the day to promote the need to urinate. You can use any other reinforcers (edible or otherwise), provided they are highly desirable and given only as reinforcement for toileting. I usually recommend a low-sugar juice brand if parents are looking for a low-sugar drink. If you are concerned with giving the child sweet drinks, start toileting with juice, then revert back to water after the toilet training process has been mastered.

12. How long can my child or student sit on the toilet during toilet training?

It depends on the child and your patience. If the child is willing to sit, you should sit with them up to their toleration level - I suggest under 10 minutes. You may set a timer to bring the child to the bathroom every 10 minutes and have the child sit on the toilet for five minutes. After this interval is complete (whether or not success is achieved), re-set the timer for another 10 minutes. Never place your child on the toilet as a punishment and avoid making the process stressful for them. You will exhaust both yourself and your child.

13. How can you train a child to have a bowel movement in the toilet?

Once the child is urinating consistently, defecation in the toilet must immediately follow. Your child is ready for this next important step once they exhibit the following signs:

● urinating in the toilet with no accidents

● holding urine

● requesting or going into the bathroom on their own to urinate

If you can check off this list, that signals

that it is a good time to introduce bowel movements in the toilet to keep up the momentum.

Start by giving your child consistent meals at consistent times (e.g., breakfast every morning at 7am/lunch at 12pm/dinner at 6pm) with foods that are high in fiber and nutrients (i.e., fresh fruit or vegetables). Please consult your pediatrician if there are issues with food.

Additionally, the child should have at least one hour of movement a day on the playground, trampoline, etc.

Once meal and activity routines are established and the child can urinate consistently, start recording the times the child typically has their bowel movement. The trick is to have the child urinate at the same time that they usually defecate. That will allow you to catch their bowel movement. Once that happens, reinforce the child with something special.

If the child is distressed by the thought of a bowel movement in the toilet, you can start by discarding their feces in the toilet whenever they void in the diaper or in their underwear. Let them see you flush the fecal matter into the toilet. This helps them to connect where their bowel movement is supposed to go. Say "bye-bye poop!", then help them flush and wash their hands.

Again, social stories are a fun, creative, and visual tool to help children make the mental shift to relieving in the toilet. Get creative! Reach out to other parents or educators who can support you, and with time, voiding in the toilet will become a new and *desirable* routine for the child.

14. When is my male child ready to stand urinating?

After the child has successfully toilet trained sitting at home or school, he is ready to start standing. This can be a little tricky – but at this point, the child should know the function of the bathroom.

When toilet training a male student, use the same verbiage and reinforcers as when the child was toilet training sitting, except have the child stand over the toilet. It can be helpful for male parents to model for the child so that they can understand the expectation. If there is no male, you can simply ask them to "pee" while they are standing up.

Again, whether it's a squirt or a dribble of urine, if it comes out of their body into the toilet, give some wait time for them to empty their bladder then reinforce. Use some wait time to raise the expectation of the amount of urine that comes out. Over time, as the child gets comfortable, he will be able to have a full stream of urine and empty his bladder completely.

15. Do I continue to toilet train when the child has outside related services/therapy or when we go out for an extended period of time?

In most cases, yes. Remember, you are creating a habit for that child that will help them to be independent. Although it is easier to keep them in a diaper "in case" the child has an accident or a bathroom is not available, it only hinders learning. If you teach them to use the bathroom only at home and at school, it will limit their independence when you go on vacations, visit friends or family, and go to games or amusement parks. So, if the child goes out with you or is with a non-parent, use the tools you learned from this book to make sure they can generalize toileting wherever they go.

16. What if nothing works?

If all efforts fail, stop the process and begin again in a few months. Connect with your special education team members for support through the process and review the tips and traits in this book to help you begin the toileting process again. The special education team, ABA therapists, agencies, and the child's pediatrician should all be involved in developing a plan for success. You are not alone.

Chapter 11: Toilet Training Tips

• **Refrain from toilet training when you are stressed or tired.** One must be mentally prepared to pour out patience and love to make the process successful for the child.

• **Read a personalized social story** for mental preparation (see Chapter 11)

• **Toilet train with a timer.** The timer holds us accountable to taking the child to the bathroom at the intervals we set – whether that be every 30 minutes or every hour. Time slips away very easily, and the timer will keep you on track.

• **Give the child *frequent* sips of juice or water to keep their bladder full.** *Remember, if there is no input, there won't be any output.* Please be cautious – If the child willingly drinks excessively, use good judgment to prohibit them from drinking to the point of overhydration, which can cause serious side effects. For a child, one or two juice boxes and some water sipped throughout the day should stimulate the urge to urinate. If you are not sure, seek advice from your pediatrician.

• **Make a diligent effort to cook healthy meals, and give the child lots of fruits and vegetables.** If your child gets sick often or has frequent diarrhea, this can throw off the toilet training process. You will be forced to keep the diaper on if the child has loose bowels.

• **Avoid standing over the child while they are on the potty as this can make them uncomfortable.** This is the time to grab a chair and sit or squat with the child. Get a book, sing songs, use a sensory toy and/or talk to them about what they will get if they urinate. This is an interactive process that can take time. Once the child is comfortable, he or she will eventually void.

• **Don't ignore the signs.** If they are crossing their legs, looking full in the belly or uncomfortable, they are probably going to urinate. This is the time to run them to the bathroom, and sit them on the toilet. They will probably want to get up, so you can gently encourage them to stay on the toilet and/or try to distract them. Sometimes letting them have access to a sensory fidget may encourage them to stay on the toilet. At some point, they won't be able to hold it. If they urinate, smile, and give them their favorite treat or toy right away. Then, help them to flush and wash their hands.

• **Start using more age-appropriate words to describe the toileting process.** Replace the words "potty" and "pee pee" with "bathroom" or "toilet" once the child has established toileting. When teaching students how to request, eventually teach and/or model "bathroom please" (using a visual) rather than "pee pee please."

- **Don't neglect hygiene**: Flushing and washing hands are important habits.

- **Finally, remember that this is a miraculous process.** You may be tempted to lose hope, but don't allow yourself to say this out loud. Maintain positive thoughts and amazing things can happen.

Reminders

o Develop goals as a parent (and/or staff) and determine why toileting is important for the child.

o Begin reading a personalized toilet training social story*.

o Make your space toilet training ready: roll carpets/rugs, cover couches and have gloves and cleaning materials readily available.

o Keep a set schedule for meals and bed times. This will regulate the child's body and help them with regular bowel movements.

o Staff/family members should set their minds for a lengthy process with many accidents in the beginning. Patience is key.

o Create a start date with the child, family and school. Parents should prepare plenty of juice boxes, underwear, pants, shirts, and a change of shoes. Be mindful to determine what reinforcer will be utilized and have it prepared.

o Prepare a data sheet* to log the child's behavior from day 1 of toilet training. Data should include time, date, interval and whether the child initiated. Designate this responsibility to one person.

o Actively use a timer daily to eliminate human error in tracking time.

o Observe and note patterns. Look for physical cues for readiness to void regardless of the timer.

o Find ways to make toileting fun (e.g., sing a song, use reinforcement for sitting and cooperating). This is very important. If the child is not motivated to go into the bathroom, you cannot toilet train them.

QR Code for Supporting Resources

*SCAN THE QR CODE TO purchase your social story and download your *free* data sheet from my Teachers Pay Teachers (TPT) account. The social story is less than $5. It is a generic social story you can download, laminate and personalize. Read it to your child daily to help him or her with the mental connection in toilet training. Please follow me and provide reviews if the social story and data sheet are effective. Your feedback is important to me.

Glossary

Autism Spectrum Disorder (ASD)

is a developmental disability caused by differences in the brain. People with ASD often have problems with social communication and interaction, and restricted or repetitive behaviors or interests.

The **Individualized Education Program (IEP)** is a written statement of our plan to provide your child with a Free and Appropriate Public Education (FAPE) in their Least Restrictive Environment (LRE).

A **reinforcer** is something that increases the likelihood that a specific behavior or response will occur. Reinforcers occur after the response or behavior that you want to increase.

Satiation is the state of having needs and desires being not only satisfied, but satisfied to a point of excess. An example of this could be a Thanksgiving dinner and the tendency to eat beyond personal need to the point of feeling stuffed, or even ill.

Social or Verbal Reinforcers: These are reinforcers

which are socially mediated by teachers, parents, other adults, and peers which express approval and praise for appropriate behavior. Comments ("Good job," "I can tell you are working really hard," "You're nice"), written approval ("Super"), and expressions of approval (nodding your head, smiling, clapping, a pat on the back) are all very effective reinforcers.

Tangible Reinforcers: This category includes edibles, toys, balloons, stickers, and awards. Edibles and toys should be used with caution. Parents may have reason to object to edibles as reinforcement (for example, if a student has a weight problem) and toys can make other students envious. Awards can be in the form of certificates, displayed work, and letters home to parents commending the student's progress. These are powerfully motivating reinforcers.

Generalization is when an individual applies something learned in a specific situation to other similar situations which is marked by progress toward therapy goals.

Prompts are instructions, gestures, demonstrations, touches, or other things that we arrange or do to increase the likelihood that children will make correct responses. In other words, a prompt is a specific form of assistance given by an adult before or as the learner attempts to use a skill.

An **Interval** is a specified length of time. Sessions can be broken up into equal parts to create intervals (Cooper,

Heron, and Heward, 2007). Examples: 30 second intervals, 5-minute intervals, 1-hour intervals. Guessing at random is not an example of an interval.

A **Social Story** presents social behaviors in the form of concrete, visual cues that make the information more digestible for children who aren't able to conceptualize an image when someone verbally explains what to do or what to expect. Social Stories are a great tool for increasing social growth in children.

Applied Behavior Analysis (ABA) is a scientific approach to understanding behavior. ABA refers to a set of principles that focus on how behaviors change, or are affected by the environment, as well as how learning takes place. The term behavior refers to skills and actions needed to talk, play, and live.

Conclusion

By following all the steps in this book and seeking support from your special education team, attaining success in training a child on the Spectrum to use the toilet will be realized. Every child, experience and situation are different with relative challenges. I firmly believe miracles will happen through perseverance. For some, it may take a few weeks or months, and for others, it may take longer. Wherever the child is on the Spectrum, you will experience small steps of success. Use the reflection section at the end of the book to record each moment, and when you look back, you will see how far you have come. My hope is that every reader of this book will have success that exceeds their dreams – with toileting and beyond. I would love to hear your stories and feedback!

QUESTIONS? PLEASE EMAIL me: toilettrainingstrategies@gmail.com. Look for me on my Instagram account: talk.toilet.training.

WRITTEN BY SABRINA VEROST, M.A. ED AND EDITED BY MONIFE G. STOUT, M.A.

Additional Reflections

66

About the Author

Sabrina Verost is a seasoned special education teacher who has toilet trained dozens of children using Applied Behavior Analysis (ABA) techniques throughout her career. This book is called ***Practical Toilet Training*** because she has helped school-aged children on the Spectrum previously deemed incapable of being toilet trained, become capable through practical and easy to follow steps. As explicitly explained in the book, with patience, reflection, and the right structures in place, you too can experience the success of ***Practical Toilet Training***.